BEHIND THE BLUE GATE

THE BLUE GATE

by CAROL ROSE

A Porcépic Book

Copyright © 1997 by Carol Rose

First Edition

All rights reserved.

No part of this book may be reproduced or transmitted in any form by any means, electronic or mechanical, including photocopying, recording or any information storage, retrieval and transmission systems now known or to be invented, without permission in writing from the publisher, except by a reviewer who may quote brief passages in a review.

This edition published by Beach Holme Publishing, #226-2040 West 12th Ave., Vancouver, BC, V6J 2G2, with the assistance of The Canada Council and the BC Ministry of Small Business, Tourism and Culture.

Cover Art © 1997 by Esther Warcov
Cover Design: Tom Osborne
Editor: Joy Gugeler

Printed and Bound in Canada by Webcom

Canadian Cataloguing in Publication Data:
Rose, Carol, 1943-
Behind the blue gate

(A Porcepic Book)
ISBN 0-88878-375-2

1. Jerusalem–Poetry. I. Title. II. Series.
PS8585.O728B44   C811'.54   C96-901061-3
PR9199.3.R5878B44 1997

for my teachers
Colette Aboulker-Muscat
& Shlomo Carlebach
who have given me a glimpse
of what lies behind the blue gate

ॐ Acknowledgments

With affection and gratitude to Di Brandt; mentor, friend and 'worthy opponent.' Our Jerusalem dialogue has certainly stretched us–renewed our faith in the power of words. To paraphrase the psalmist, "may the words of our mouths and the meditations of our hearts be acceptable to You, Creator of Shalom."

To 'motherpoet,' Anne Szumigalski, my heartfelt appreciation. Her wisdom, talent, generosity and skill have enriched my life.

Many thanks to Carol Shields for her guidance, encouragement and counsel.

To the Sage Hill Writing Experience, thanks for the opportunity to write, undisturbed and inspired.

Ari Averette, Marianne Cerilli, Mimi Feigelson, Elinor Johns, Judy Goldsmith, Sylvia Legris, Mindy Lofchick, Shira Waldman and most especially, Kate Bitney and Joan Turner for their friendship and ongoing support.

To Avi, Carnie, Kliel, Or-Nistar and Adira for their patience and love. For Neal . . . always there . . . with a listening ear and an open heart.

Thanks also to the women and men who shared their healing stories with me.

To Ulla Ryum, thank you for 'broadening my world' and for sensitively translating some of my poems into Danish.

Many thanks to Esther Warcov for her beautiful cover illustration, to Barbara Gingold for her blue gate photographs, and to Joe Connor for taking my portrait.

A special thank you to Joy Gugeler for her gentle, collaborative efforts in bringing this book to completion, and to Beach Holme Publishing for their faith in the manuscript.

I would also like to express my appreciation to the Manitoba Arts Council and the Winnipeg Arts Advisory Council for their generous support.

Several of these poems have appeared in *Jerusalem 3000: An Anthology of Jewish Canadian Writing* (Vehicule, 1996), *Celebrating the Moon: A Rosh Chodesh Anthology* (Jason Aronson, 1995), *The Rabinical Assembly Holocaust Reader* (The Jewish Theological Seminary, 1995), *Beyond Bad Times* (Snowapple Press, 1993,) *Drop Out* (Rhinocerotic Press, 1993) and *Vintage 92* (League of Canadian Poets, 1992). They have also appeared in the following journals: *Canadian Women's Studies, Contemporary Verse 2, Dandelion, Other Voices, Parchment, Praire Fire, Possibilitiis, Quarry, The Amethyst Review, The Wascana Review, Whetstone, Women's Education des Femmes, Zygote.* A number of poems included have also been broadcast on "Arts Encounters" (CBC Radio), "Sundayscope" (CKY TV) and "The Jewish Connection" (Videon TV).

Table of Contents

Whenever I Return............ 9

The Crones.................. 33

There's No Telling........... 49

Making Love in the Air........ 65

Behind the Blue Gate......... 83

Whenever I Return

☙

ஐ Jerusalem: another version of the story

(for Di Brandt)

i wanted to tell you more
but you were leaving
the next day
with your daughters
for a place
that doesn't always appear
friendly to girlchildren
so i focused my telling
on that part of the tale
that would allow you
to take them
down narrow streets
that cross themselves
in filigreed patterns
praying your way
would be paved with dates
pomegranates figs
& women who grow
& bake & sell in the open
hoping you'd feed
on delicacies
Yeminite Bedouin Persian
embroidery   dances
songs in threepart harmony
not a folklorama
but a taste of the spirit
is what i wished you

i suppose i could have told you
(in the words of the ten spies)
that *this is a land*
that devours
its inhabitants
i chose another version
of the story instead

ಐ for chrystos

your poetry is
so compelling
that i
squeeze
your books
into suitcases
loaded with gifts
for loved ones
in israel
pack them
especially
for me to read
on cool mauve
jerusalem evenings
on ben yehuda street
where i sip bitter
arabic coffee & listen
to my people
speak the language
of their ancestors
even though
they never heard
a word of hebrew
in their parent's home

perhaps it's the longing
i hear
the longing
for menominee phrases

that makes me want
to bring you here
to this promised land
where ancient words
are reborn in the mouths
of little children
& the screams
of beaten ones
are transformed
into song

whenever i return

whenever i return
to jerusalem
it's like meeting
an old lover again

the joy
intensity passion
awakening

in trembling light
shimmering
topaz pink
against the dark
desert sand

coming
out of exile

☙ here morning explodes

cacophonous   sonic
booms pierce the air
clotheslines play violin
to the beat of women
pounding persian rugs
on stone   pedlars chant
"alter zachin" "sabras"
overhead doves
tap castanet
wings   pink & gold
in the sunlight   metal
shutters click click
their lids   alleys
hum a merchants' tune
hebrew arabic russian
in the valley echoes
call the faithful
to worship or war
a new day in Jerusalem

ಬ **The Wall**

In Jerusalem
I always come
Face to face
With my longing

It never fails
The hunger   desire
The frantic search
For doorways

I seek Your heart
Find only cracks
Stuffed with prayers

I become a prayer
Folded   tattered
Small enough
To fit Your wounds

I shape myself
In secret hollows
Cling mosslike
To Your ancient contours

Body on body
We lovers loosen
Rocks that separate us

In the morning
Only doves and beggars
Come to witness
Your return to stone

prayer

in Jerusalem
mothers press

their bodies
against stone

grow wild
like moss

in crevices
of jagged rock

melt like
anointing oil

in the heat
of ancient walls

too narrow
to admit anything

but the prayer
for peace

the wailing
on the other side

৪০ hallel

(a song of praise)

the taste
of your
tear soaked
stones stays
on my tongue
not tied
to palate
my right hand
not withered
holds fast
& remembers
Jerusalem
where men
preen their
prayershawls
like peacocks
as women wail
in labour
birthing
songs
of hope
under a new
moon

☙ under a fingernail

i come to this ancient wall at night
stand silent
under a fingernail
of new moon

jerusalem's black magic
sky opens
splinters
into rainbows of colour

stars chime
a hundred lutes echo in the rock
& in the caverns of my heart
a flutter of doves

always in my eye

>   in the rosegold
>   of morning
>   it's hard to tell
>   if this place is
>   of my dreams

jerusalem

>   always in my eye
>   pulsing
>   at the edge
>   of everything
>   i see

an amber sun

>   reflecting
>   on stone
>   whatever
>   the landscape
>   this light

searing

ஓ in the desert again

i write home say *i'm in the desert again* (though
i'm not sure why) feel sent like my ancestors open
lavender skies (rimmed apricot) canopy my head
fire-red ocotillo blossoms glow in the sunlight (are not
consumed) i never feel lost here   know this place
(by heart) this place where stories are born   majestic
as the mountains huge breasts nurturing heaven
hugging the horizon (vermillion against blue) these
mountains orient me (camelback & old squawpeak)
these motherhills guide me past cactus & decaying
skulls i encounter history eternal wandering &
woundedness (familiar)   shifting under my feet
each mesa leads me backwards   carries me through
the labyrinth of legend   ancient map of sorrow
& joy   scoring my bone to the marrow

☙ so much life curdling

there's so much blood in these judean hills
so much life curdling among the cactus
where flowers once promised to grow
the earth turned copper/brown
an old wrinkled skin
drying in the unbearable heat of war
losing herself daily

passover eve

blood on the door
posts a warning
there's change about
a splitting
bodies of water foam madly
moonlight tides flood new shores
on the edge of riverbanks
womanspirit drummers chant
bathed in silver
they dance

☙ even the rocks

everything
is significant
here
even the rocks
hold memory
moriah
the red sea
sinai
all etched
in jerusalem
stone
fragments
of our past
they resonate
with story
sing
our wandering
these rocks
rebuild
our cities
in the hands
of our enemies
kill
our young
erase
our future

ಬಿ at the Rawdah Cafe

(for the Israeli rescue team on the date of a mud slide in East Jerusalem March 1, 1992)

it doesn't really matter that you've never
been welcome before
at the Rawdah Cafe
where burial grounds come crashing
down the mountain in a storm
smash the roof of this old city hang-out
break down walls & grab the living
where they sit playing cards or planning a revolt
on this snowy afternoon in Jerusalem
it doesn't really matter that you've come here now
to the Rawdah Cafe
to help clear away skeletons of ancestors
some who may have murdered members
of your own family it doesn't really matter
as long as you get through
to the ones who are still struggling
to stay alive & sane beneath the mud
that covers this place

ಬ spinning to drown out evil
(Hebron - Purim, 1994)

it shouldn't surprise you that my heart
is fissured   fractured into millions of
jagged pieces   bleeding all over
the floor   the walls   staining everything
with morse code dots & dashes
signaling H-E-L-P
there is no place to go   no
single friend   country   sanctuary   no
roads out or in   only the half-darkened
light of *shabbat*   i can't go to synagogue
today   wait at home for family to return
community seems a burden   can't be sure
of where my people stand   how could this
happen in *adar*   the hebrew month of
auspiciousness & blessing   jewish children
dressed in purim attire   their mardi gras
noise-makers spinning to drown out evil
outside the tombs of our shared ancestors
hundreds of *abui-bui*clad women   wailing
for their dead   everyone afraid to enter
everyone afraid to pray   in this land
littered with hate

ೞ election day - israel - 1992

i arrive in jerusalem
in time for the elections
everyone is out   rushing
to work & back   rushing
to designated stalls
identity cards in hand
rushing to cast ballots
even those who can't read
vote for change   for peace

if it wasn't for the identity cards
i'd swear we were in synagogue
rushing to hear the last blast
on the ram's horn on yom kippur eve
praying for our lives   our land

on the west bank
the bbc announcer reports
three israeli merchants were murdered . . .

a gift to the new government
from terrorists
who register their vote
in blood

❧ a parable

the newscaster recites a parable on the radio
(following his latest report about hebron)
it's tells the tale of a spider who wants
to cross the river jordan on the back
of a beautiful swan   the swan refuses
saying *you'll sting me as i fly*
the spider protests *why would i do that?*
if i did, we'd both die   the swan agrees
& they cross the holy waters together   in
mid-air the spider bites the swan *why*
did you betray me? moans the wounded
bird *i don't know*   the spider replies
but you must remember, this is the
middle-east & anything is possible here

there must be another end to this tale
another version only women can write
I'm remembering the old stories   stories
grandmothers' told about spiders   how
they were sacred   could weave new
realities out of their own bodies   create
a new world   how swans were really lovely birds
graceful creatures   searching for home

ಬಿ accord
(September 13, 1993)

somehow i thought that day would be different
that day on the lawn of the white house
the whole world watching
enough blood finally enough blood enough tears
woman wailing no more
the dead & unborn rising finally rising
but it wasn't like that at all

men dressed for war standing for peace
the whole world watching
only words without warmth & hands
reluctant   stretching beyond time
toward a dream an old dream eternal
without warmth only hands
stretching beyond time
the dead & unborn wailing

on the lawn of the white house
only words

❧ dialogue

you read from your new politicized work
PLO sympathies show up in your
Jerusalem poems
your voice trembles
as it always does
when you come up against something
you feel   passionately

> in the audience my heart stretches
> tauter than drumskin
> it vibrates with ancestral pain
> trembles
> as it always does
> when i come up against something
> i feel   passionately

when you leave the stage
there's no olive branch
you simply say
we need dialogue

> i agree
> the whole story must be told
> Jerusalem
> in Her many voices

ʮ i need

i need to tell you
that my fears are real
even if they conflict
with your image
of Jews
& our old testament

i need to talk to you
about the land
about embodying a dream
even as the Palestinians
voice their claim

i need to be seen
not as a metaphor
for suffering
not as a perpetrator
of violence

i need to be heard
even when my anger
my exile
frightens you

i need to know
you are listening

༄ elijah

i can't wait to get back to canada to tell joan
elinor di to tell neal that i met elijah
driving his chariot on the bethlehem road
i can't wait to tell them how he took me
in the heat of july his cab weaving
through date palms & cypress
light spinning wheels turning
as we sped through the streets of jerusalem
how we talked about war & his children & mine
how he turned off the road my heart pounding
as he pointed to an inscription on the doorway
of an old arab house how he read me the message
"allah lives here in these gates you will find god"
how he prayed for an end to the killing
in arabic/hebrew how we prayed together
in that dark narrow lane
how we turned the air golden

The Crones

☙

❧ when women study the bible

he asks, "just what is it that you want to do to the bible, anyway? do you think that you can change it to suit your own whim, your mood, your particular view of reality? it's just amazing how people try to bend history to meet their own needs"

"isn't it though," i reply

ಏ pillar of salt

you stand resplendent in the sun
an ancient shrine   relic from a cult
like your name   long forgotten
there's mystery in your womanform
cast in crystal or made of tears
when not even ten in His image
could be called worthy   & you were
left shimmering in the sand
witness to a time
when looking back was sacred

ೞ recalling sinai

(Exodus XIX:14 - 16) "And Moses went down from the mount unto the people, and sanctified the people; and they washed their garments. And he said to the people; 'Be ready for the third day; *come not near a woman.*' And it came to pass on the third day, that there were thunders and lightnings and a thick cloud upon the mount, and the voice of a horn exceeding loud; and all the people that were {allowed} in the camp trembled."

> what do you remember about that night, daughter
> not the images carefully planted in your head
> arranged in neat little rows like holes dug for beans
>
> what did you see in moonlight, sister
> before flashes of lightning & rumble of thunder
> secreted away your vision
> curled it in on itself like a folded shawl
>
> what did you hear blanketed in fog, mother
> what muffled voice called you, still calls you
> in mountain mists & waking dreams
>
> leaves your skin glowing
> face radiant as moses

☙ Miryam

i've watched
these women
for years
observing
their rites
i've seen them
sparkling
in moonlight
their limbs
coated in
sugarwater
hardening
into a second
skin that rips
hair from legs
mound thighs
as it's peeled
from their bodies
by a priestess
i've smelled
the henna potion
used to redden
skin against
the evileye
protection
from the curse
of barrenness

i've heard
their singing
soulful sweet
as the darkness
recedes and
the morningstar
comes to waken
Pharaoh's daughter
and her maids
to a monthly
ritual in the Nile
i've come to know
their mysteries
tied to moontime
and the swelling
of the sea
i wait
at the mouth
of the river
undulating
with the tides
i've grown wise
in the art
of midwifery
delivering
Moses
the child
to the womb
of their Motherwaters

ಐ Jochebed

dearest child
I wonder if I'm dreaming
this night
this last night with you
sleeping
my breast in your mouth
close
as if we were one body
still
in a few hours you'll be
gone
taken from me in a chariot
of reeds
mud & pitch the only arms
to hold you
safe against the sea
of death
it's all been planned
every detail
if the tides are right
you'll find
a circle of women
waiting
to take you in
their gift
from the Mothergod
one
they've been dreaming of
all night

ೞ Bithya*

i carry
my *ankh*
to the river
wait for
morninglight
to cast a circle
around its
golden loop
i step inside
face east
disrobe
chant
offering songs
to Mother Nile
i pray
She will swell
overflow
i leave
Her sacred waters
refreshed
return to shore
dress in
carnelian robes
a *tijet*
at my throat
i hear
a conch cry
women run

dance
carry a basket
in their arms
they shout
    "a gift
     from the Gods
     a gift
     from the Mother"
i look
find the answer
to my prayers
in a weave
of mud & reeds

the Talmud identifies Bithya (or Batya) as the princess of Egypt who rescues the infant, Moses, from the Nile and adopts him as her son

lilith

men fear you   hang amulets
on babies' cribs & red ribbons

from the bedposts
of boychildren

who grow long hair
to fool you

sages chant secret incantations
against your return at night

they sleep with holy books
under their mattresses

face east   rest
only on the left side of the body

they never eat garlic or onion
before going to bed

never touch their wives
during bleeding times

never never look
at the holy place of birth

lilith women never learn about you
never even hear your name

your holy place of birth bleeds
women look at it   chant incantations

face east
grow long hair & feast

write holy books   at night
return to power

                                                  echo
                                               location

i scan the deep
   like a dolphin
     listen for
         echo
           locating
              clicks

              search the seas
       for sisterlife

               beneath the tides
          a conch
        parts pink
       quivers
at my touch

          releases
            lilith's voice

                 primal
                    it resonates
                         sings

hers is the beauty

hers is the beauty of Dark
lagoons
of ebony
of moonspEckled hair
& eyes
nuMinous as night
her mOuth
aNisesweet
& tart
tonguE
fearleSs strong
name
whispered
in shadowS
still

fourmothers

we gather together
under a new moon
to name them
Sarah
Rebekkah
Rachel
Leah
to tell their tales
as they were told
to us   deception
jealousy
rivalry
shame
the wrong testament
carved in stone
crumbles in nightair
falls to dust
waits for moonlight
to resurrect
a narrative reborn
in the mouths of women
sings of wisdom
courage
daring
pain

she lives alone

she waits
for her dreams
to give her direction
follows internal rules

she divines
in the ancient way
dances with prophets
discovers new shores

she lives alone

in harmony
with the seasons
in communion
with herself

Lamentations

Ancient Mother whom we call
Y'RUSHA/ SHALEM/ SHALOM
inheritance/ wholeness/ peace
your prophets blame you
for your pain   say lewdness
stripped your jasmine waistband
of its boughs   your breast
is seared from suckling
too many lovers on one side
guilty   they all cry   *harlot   whore*
your worm infested belly lies accused
your flesh rent inside out
by rape   your womb's grotesque
miscarriage of the young in war
keeps you still   the victim

the crones of jerusalem

three times daily your people Israel
gathers for prayer   chants
ancient psalms you don't understand
studies sacred books you can't read

you join them wearing floral housecoats
tattered slippers take you to your place
on the women's side of the sanctuary

you sit behind veils   separate
even from them   the younger women
who go to school   learn the complex laws
speak the holy tongue

you gesture a blessing
kiss aging fingertips to the sky
sprinkle the room with rosewater
"Ha Shem Yeracheim
may compassion flow from the divine womb"
the only prayer you know
perfumes the air

There's No Telling

kitchens of my childhood

my aunt gussie the neighbourlady from across
the dumbwaiter wall where garbage & gossip
gathered daily knew everything i mean every-
thing about us closer than kin she helped mom
find her first lump examined her breast right
in her kitchen the day i started to bleed she
was there too slapped me in the face this time
in our kitchen never said a word just smacked me
i wondered about that about why my becoming a
women made her act so crazy did she know about
her father *pops* who grabbed me every chance he
got even before i started to bleed stuck his tongue
down my throat in the kitchen hers or ours it didn't
seem to matter *where* he was old & hungry never
said a word just grabbed me made me feel like a
dumbwaiter full of other people's garbage i
wondered if anyone ever tried to slap him in the
face or if gussie felt the fear that grew
cancerous in the kitchens of my childhood

in the blue light

so there's this room with a blue light
over my head   a blue light that i
always check to see if it's still there
& if i am   in this room that i can never
find in the actual floorplan of my grand-
father's house   his & not her's   though
she's there   in the doorway   when i
wake to the sounds of my four year old
screams   & hers   as i kick opa's chest
screaming & kicking & pushing his chest
at the foot of my bed   what is he doing
there anyway   what are his hands doing
on my belly   my belly   she always says
he's stroking you awake   rubbing your
belly you naughty child   kicking at opa
his heart so frail   he's sick you know
& all he wants is to wake you   lovingly
stroke your belly   & you   you just keep
on kicking & screaming   you naughty
child   opa says nothing in the blue light

there's no telling

there's no telling
what will happen
when the memories
start
they just flow
in a rhythm
all their own
surfacing
in images
vaguely connected
stirring up
feelings
left behind
in tenements
where girls played
safely
with ginny dolls
far from adult rules
powerful
until a man
joined their game
changing
"make-believe"
into fantasies
of his own
no
there's no telling
when the memories

start
they just come
when they will
with their secrets
intact
    and
        breaking

alone in his bed

she looks into a mirror
sees her future
blackened eyes
swollen lips
every Saturday night
another fight

she shows him the mirror
asks for release
angrily he helps her
pack her bags
takes another drink
grabs the mirror
tosses it out

he curses   bends
to clear away the pieces
cuts his hand
on broken glass
lies down
alone in his bed
and bleeds

it says remember

snatches of memory
haunt me   drive me
crazy

fuzzy bits & pieces
snowflakes   feathers
they float
above my bed
in dreams   they dance
i writhe
in pain   know these images
belong   forget why

one dream
multiplies
it says
remember

the call

you'd say
you can't reach
out anymore
your body tires too easily
to roll over & start again

ringing with hunger
you grab the phone
it's harmless
you say

ruby says
you raped her last night
entered her dreams

she says
you came into her bed
uninvited licking the air
for contact your tongue
assaulting her ear

she says
you hung up
& there was nothing
to cradle but fear

in the morning you return
a shining star you leave
the darkness behind
for ruby
& other women
who hear your voice
in every call

in my own image

i've been altered
by the surgeon's knife
carved in two
my womb lifted
from my body
i'm left empty

i've been altared
forced to rearrange myself
around vacant space
sacred space
like in the beginning
using the void

ex nihilo
i fashion the world
in my own image
call it by name
place it
in a garden
of my own choosing

body images

(for Joan Turner)

you massage me into a dream
the sea & an old ship   i'm
a fish slithering beneath
the ship's worn belly searching
for a rope to raise its anchor
i pull it up with my teeth
release it from the depths
you talk to me   whisper something
Karen always says   stroke my cheeks
dig into bones for hidden tears
you remind me to breathe   i exhale
sighs so old & distant they sound
like someone else's cry in me
i open my mouth & pain comes out
in trembling waves   you touch
my body lovingly caressing sinew
muscle tissue   i uncoil softening
in the blue green light   a sea hag
clings to the curve of the anchor
changing as she rises into a wolf
then a bear standing on hind legs
totems bringing health endurance
power   i grow   into myself   taller
rounder exquisite in the wisdom
& caring of your hands

you stand colt-like   unsure

your body remembers the child
you open your eyes
 separate moist lashes
cry years of numbness awake
shake as you get up & run
from memories that bleed
into your quivering limbs
you stand colt-like   unsure
you walk back into life
wiser than the woman
who began this journey
your *manyselvestogether*
join in a sacred dance

growing pains

you said you had no right
i was too young to know
what you meant, your body
holding me close as you spoke
i thought i could grow up
quickly that way, near to you,
in your shadow, not knowing
the danger of being there,
at the edge of your humanity,
where your needs were all
that mattered, and my pain
lay forgotten in the lap
of the women projected
onto me by your hunger
i still remember the promises,
and the girl/child who died
waiting for them to come true

gift from the muse

(for Carol Shields)

you introduce
yourself
show me
a treasure
box   small
golden   coated
with enamel
flowers
a tiny chest
gift
from the muse
it hides
your words
keeps them safe
until they
like butterflies
are ready to fly

breaking the rules

    when   they soar
       lore   of light
         instead of   and full
         law   wings moist
          guides   butterfly
           there's a   they grow
           gentle   of others
             breaking   run by the will
               (on the inside)   in a world
              rules   themselves
                    test

ms.

i've learned to live without you to love
myself again i toughen my heart rock
myself awake i've learned to separate your life
from mine no sticky yellow traces streak my egg-
white foam of womandreams i move about
unscrambled often in moonlight shadows
of you shock my eyes insanely open as you rise
from memory i've learned that love dissolves in pillows
& only rage lifts my head from the bed I made & lie
in still

Making Love in the Air

❧

❧ i see myself coming

as though in a dream i see myself coming
closer to who i am   i move   melt
become liquid   in the bed of our longing
i find my love   know my beauty   taste
my own sweetness on fingertips
locked shut since our parting   your tongue
draws circles inside my mouth   i explode
become pure light   discover my power
your passion awakens   meets the fullness
of my own   your thighs hold me
i reconstruct myself at their root

ॐ gifts

(for neal)

i return to genesis bookstore with
the serpent you bought for my ear

afraid to lose it in the tangles
of my hair i choose instead

a pendant of the goddess carved
in two half moons of bronze   i wear it

between my breasts & feel its ancient
power each time i move or take a breath

it's amazing how we gift each other -
you bring me a snake waiting for love

to uncoil, i exchange it for a symbol
open at its core

ଏ palmistry

                                                                                             of a rose
                                                                                             i search
                            you chose   the patterns engraved
                            to print it   in your palm in the flesh
i find   open   read a poem beneath
a photo   vulnerable   the skin
copy of   as the centre   a radiance
your hand
wonder why   i never
                                                                                            knew
                                                                                            your pulse
                                                                                            in shades
                                                                                            of muted light

ஓ i wait

for your tongue
to slide
past my lips
circle
the inside
of my mouth
coax honey
from deep
in my womb

I open my throat
in songs
summoned
by the urging
of your kiss

☯ making love in the air

we're like acrobats
turning over & over
reluctantly
releasing our hold
passing each other on
to higher & higher rungs
making love in the air

ᛒ they talk theology instead

has your passion ever been met ?

she probes past
permitted terrain   opens the soul
exposes the chaos he fears

what i've done is fight   love
my children   write   keeps me
out of the dark zone   the night
sweats   nazis & demons far
from my bed

hardly the answer she imagined
they talk theology instead   angels
dance on the tips of their questions
beings of light   whirling at the edge

❦ last night she

last night she
sat outside
her négligée
fondling the lace
still moist
with love
left behind
in its web
she put it on
allowing passion
to embroider
tiny patterns
on her breasts
weaving rosebuds
on the inside
of her thighs

☋ there's nothing left for us

our love is like the moon
frail & shy with new light
then round, full to brimming
until it falls, again, into darkness.

there's nothing left for us
to do, together
only ride the sky
to the end of night.

☯ before you return

i prepare myself like a bride
bathe in oil bubbles delight
every pore   i dress with an eye
toward your undressing
sense your caress in the silk
of my gown your touch in the lace
the sheets on our bed come alive
before you return the scent
of your skin in their folds

෴ alchemy

i make you my muse
take pain
& facet it into song
lift it like a jewel
to the stars
offer it to the one
who turns everything
to gold

ஜ inspiration

i find you in bed with my lover in dreams
in conversation you quiver between us

i read you in fables poetry tales
paintings splash you delicately
in colour line movement the body holds you
gracefully dances you to the sea music
sings you to the birds flies you
south in winter keeps you
warm in wingpits close to the heart

you rise with the sun dawn at first light glow
in the nightsky   the moon
caresses you sends you
back to earth on meteorite tails rivulets of dew
on the lips of rosebuds your breath luminescent

૪ი i need you closer still

i'm flooded with light
colour sound with the scent
of your spices on my skin
coriander cumin *zhatah*
jerusalem marketplace
of sensual delights
i need you closer still
brand me   carve your name
into my flesh   make me your own
impregnate me with song
i long to birth your heart
in peace

behind separate doors

what we probably should do is pass the night together,
hold each other, as children do, tight until the dark
subsides   but we won't, afraid of entanglement, afraid
of expectations, afraid . . . "did you see that one, there,
exploding over head?" we watch the sky for meteorites,
drink scotch, share our failures, our fears   we rake
the powerful over coals, celebrate joys, family, a few
friend . the meaning of things is what intrigues us–
the inner, deeper, truer– the nameless   we mount it
from different angles though, spark each other
"there's nothing sexier than god," one of us says. we hug,
exchange a few sighs, return to our rooms   behind
separate doors, we steam our bodies, write about love

☯ resurrecting the dead

the night your mother died we rolled around
the livingroom floor   resurrecting the dead
years between us   resurrecting the passion
everything reverting back to what it had been
before we sank into numbness   the morning
sticky with latte'   mouths dripping honey

ಬ scenting You

i carry Your scent in a crystal jar
jasmine blossoms sand & sage

i open the lid   especially
in winter   sniff the air

i discover Your smell
in tall prairie grass

catch a hint of Your musk
on the flesh of new wheat

even corn reminds me
i inhale Your perfume in its hair

ಬ flowering passion

cut from your roots
alstromeria
half a world away
from your home
you tremble
in fluorescent light
quiver
in the showcase
where i stand
unable to warm you

tender aloe
what strange fate
mingles
in a flowershop
window
your healing
sweetens the air
forces me open
i grow pink & gold
with desire

Behind the Blue Gate

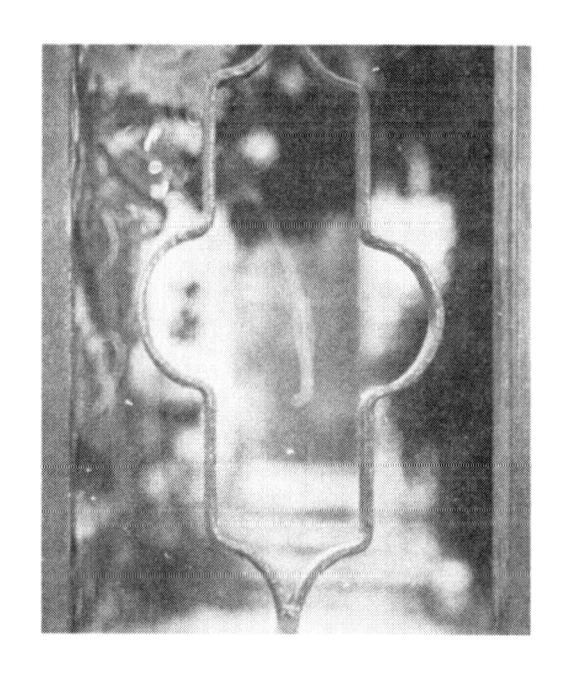

☞

೮つ anne's story

(for Anne Szumigalski)

she sits on the sofa her cane
balanced against the wall nearest
the frontdoor her eyes turned in-
ward to the rock she carries in her
chest wherever she goes victims
of war still telling their tales
fifty years later
little brown bars
washing the wounded
human flesh turned to soap
she wonders if her hands
will ever feel clean again
or if the rock will finally lift
when she tells what she knows

the goblet

(for Kate Bitney)

do you feel things? you ask taking a ruby red goblet from the china cabinet behind you. *i mean do you sense things, get information from handling objects ?* i don't know, i reply. *here, touch this* you say, handing me the cup. *close your eyes & feel.* the glass is warm in my hands, surprisingly warm. it feels like a wound, bloody & full of pain. where does it come from? *it's a gift from my father. he brought it back from the old country, kept it in his suitcase for years, never took it out or even mentioned it, just gave it to me on my wedding night. what do you suppose it was used for?* it reminds me of our passover chalice, the one we used on sedar nights. a blue crystal cup saved for prophet elijah, the cup of redemption, only this one is red & full of sadness. *i wonder if it was a family heirloom, something he needed to bring back & pass on to me, his eldest child, something from his past. michelle says that it cuts into her skin, leaves a tiny triangle in the centre of her palm, hurts her whole body everytime she touches it. she thinks it was a sabbath glass, a jewish ritual cup torn from its home.*

i feel it again, smell fire & death. its half-lotus shape burns my hands. i see a torch, war, a pogrom. it's been through a pogrom, i say. *i only sense sharp edges,* you say. *it needs to be cleared. did i ever tell you that my mother said that dad told her he was jewish? only once, when they were courting. it didn't seem to matter. mom just let him talk. he needed to, it was just after the war, he was healing, needed to sort things out. a man with no country, no family. mom just listened, but he never said it again. years later they tried to find people with the same polish name as dad's. the only people with that name were jews. they stopped looking. this goblet needs to be cleared. do you know any jewish rituals for cleansing? i'm sure that's what it needs. it's what i need, too,* you say.

‽ warsaw roundabout

there's not a brick
of the old ghetto left
only carousel horses

                            (on the other side
                              of the river)

& ghosts
dropping in & out
of view
like children
riding ash
coloured ponies

                            (to hurdy-gurdy
                              calliope tunes)

bobbing up & down
laughter rising
like flames

                            (no one ever thought
                              to stop the music)

survivors

every night she went to bed
    with fear
        her father's arm
            tatooing nightmares
                on the pillow near her head
                    where he sat telling stories
                        from the death camps

if she ever cried
    enough
    enough
        he'd say
            you think you're suffering
            remember the children
            of Auschwitz
                then he'd kiss her
                goodnight
                    the smell of gas still on his lips

❧ tears splintering the night

(for adira tiferet rose)

after dinner our friends go to see shindler's list.
you want to go too. *how will i ever know?*
i want to go with them, i want to know everything
your eight year old voice trembles. how
many times will i have to repeat this story? how
can i tell my children the truth without passing on
the nightmares, abandoned suitcases, sabbbath candle-
sticks blackening in ss warehouses, photographs, hundreds
of vanishing faces, their eyeglasses mountain-high, their
shoes piled to heaven, jewish soles waiting for owners
to return, waiting at train stops & deathcamps. maybe
tonight i'll just tell you about the bread, challah loaves
stuffed with gems, swallowed in haste (like passover
matzah). maybe then you'll understand why i can't let you
go, eyes shining like diamonds, tears splintering the night

∾ separation

(for Or- Nistar)

when you first separated
from me i had no choice
all i could do was hold you
on my belly   stroke you   coo
until the cord stopped pulsing
i lay there
as others severed
our bodies
your father stood witness
interrupting
only to welcome you
with magic words
blessings of his own

one week later you were taken
from me again
claimed by the community
initiated with the knife
your father handed to the agent
of tradition   while i watched
your brothers   frightened
by the blood   the crowd
i tried to comfort them
tried to say something
about this rite that marked you
forever   a member of the tribe
of abraham   no ram
to take the pain

when you were three
we cut your hair   ritualized
your entry into boyhood
used a blade again
your brothers huddled
afraid of scissors
i baked cookies
in the shape of letters
an ancient alphabet
to give you food
for thought   help you learn
the power of words

today you leave for school
no ceremony to announce
the change   no crowds
your brothers gone
a baby sister sleeping
in the room that once was yours
no words   sweet cakes
no instruments of steel
no arms wide enough
to stave the ache   of separation

☙ It's Customary To Cry

for Carnie & Paulie
June 25, 1995

It's customary to cry
At weddings
Broken glass
From the marriage cup
Clings to our shoes
Pierces the ground
Transforms it
Into Jerusalem
Wherever we are
The sharp pain of exile
Shatters our dreams
As we stand
Under the canopy
Waiting

ಉ Questioning

(for Mimi)

She's been trained to question   ask   inquire
to wrestle answers from husks of complacency
peeling away layers   raw   bloody
never allowing protective scarring
She lives in Jerusalem
& riddle solving has a long history there
developed over centuries
by bearded rabbis searching for meaning
in a single word   in its location
or in the number of times it appears
on the page   *People of the Book*
seeking answers from ancient scrolls
unravelling truths   letter by letter
from parchment punctuated
by the blank spaces
where her questions originate
her own questions
about what seems to be missing
what appears by innuendo alone
or about what is not yet written
This exegetic process
she has learned so well
calls attention to the emptiness she feels
inside   each time the sacred lore is opened
to the oft times nameless
& frequently shapeless lives of women
whose stories are recorded
in only the faintest ink

this father

this father of daughters
does he cry when he recites
the morning blessing
thanking his God
for *"not creating him a woman"*
when he reads from the holy scrolls
does his throat bleed
with screams of protest
against those who silence women
in his house of prayer
what does he see when he studies
page after page of commentary
does he go blind
looking for women
who are named
do his eyes water
cleansing his sacred texts
this father of daughters
does he tell his fellows
that they are guilty
of injustice
in God's name
does he speak the truth

☯ god the mother

you're the theologian the one
who seeks the face & speaks
the name you're the one
who writes about mountain-
tops & depth of wells & primal
pairs & being filled & coated
with holiness you're the one
who teaches preaches shows
the way so why get angry when
 i ask about god the mother why
tremble & drop your gaze say
this question is political not
spiritual say anyway she died
when i was ten & i replaced her
say this is not for me god the father
will do maybe the friend but never
never the mother say anyway you
know i don't believe in a personal
god leave me wondering who it is
you really pray to every morning
your voice full of pain & longing

ঞ Morning Prayer

                Like a bride
              I wrap my heart
            Seven times around
              In ribbons of light
              An obsidian jewel
              Affixes my soul
           And directs its sight

I will betroth You to me forever
I will betroth You to me with tears,
I will betroth You to me with song
And You shall know love

The Sabbath

this is where
i come alive
this every friday night
at sunset   with candles
welcoming me
from weekday cares

this is where
i reconnect
with children   lover
friends   a world at war
with itself   my resting
place of wine & loaves

this double portion
of long ago   gathered
around my sofa
with a good book
& loved ones praying
for peace in Jerusalem

this is where
i return   always
to the Sabbath
dancing my way back
to ancestral chambers   joy
encircling my heart

࿇ eagle i

(for joe connor)

the sun breaks orange
ochre mauve
runs red
along the shoreline
spreads purple
across the lake
a shiver
of silvery blue
unsoftens my vision
i glide
darken the surface
shatter
the morning waters
with my hunger

☙ caressing me as i soar

i try so hard to face your death
to leave the nest you wove
intact   on top of the jasmine
planted forty years ago
in a new land
i want to go
dancing through forests
on other shores
as you'd have me do
flying alone   to heights
you prepared me for
i want to grow eagle wings
wide enough to hold your smile
your eyes keeping me on course
as i circle the skies   your hair
in the wind   caressing me
as i soar

behind the blue gate

(for Colette)

everything i've tried to understand comes
streaming into this garden behind the blue gate

a sprinkling of light, a luminous presence
an instant of exchange, then a vague sense
of two hands holding my heart, caressing it
placing it gently among the wildflowers

ೞ married, forever

i place myself in the garden
between jasmine & pomegranate
a fragrant light envelops me
anoints me with song
i inhale the breath of trees
sprout green
between my toes
roots deep & thick
burrow their way into soil
i am a bough
moist with white blossoms
quivering in the sweet scented air
of jerusalem
married, forever, to this land
my ancestors named holy

CAROL ROSE was nominated in 1996 for the John Hirsch Award for the most promising Manitoba writer. She has toured with Mennonite poet Di Brandt performing their dialogical work *Occupied Territories: An Argument in Poetry*. Rose received second prize in the Stephen Leacock Poetry competition in 1994, has been published widely in anthologies and literary journals and is a member of the board of *Prairie Fire*. She lives in Winnipeg with her husband and is the mother of five children. She spends her summers in Jerusalem working with Jewish artists.